DRESSING UP
DEATH

GOD'S UNBECOMING
FIT OF GRIEF

DEBBIE VANDERSLICE

WESTBOW
PRESS®
A DIVISION OF THOMAS NELSON
& ZONDERVAN

This book is a work of non-fiction. Unless otherwise noted, the author and the publisher make no explicit guarantees as to the accuracy of the information contained in this book and in some cases, names of people and places have been altered to protect their privacy.

WestBow Press books may be ordered through booksellers or by contacting:

WestBow Press
A Division of Thomas Nelson & Zondervan
1663 Liberty Drive
Bloomington, IN 47403
www.westbowpress.com
844-714-3454

Because of the dynamic nature of the Internet, any web addresses or links contained in this book may have changed since publication and may no longer be valid. The views expressed in this work are solely those of the author and do not necessarily reflect the views of the publisher, and the publisher hereby disclaims any responsibility for them.

Any people depicted in stock imagery provided by Getty Images are models, and such images are being used for illustrative purposes only. Certain stock imagery © Getty Images.

Scripture quotations are from the ESV® Bible (The Holy Bible, English Standard Version®), copyright © 2001 by Crossway, a publishing ministry of Good News Publishers. Used by permission. All rights reserved.

Scripture quotations taken from The Holy Bible, New International Version® NIV® Copyright © 1973 1978 1984 2011 by Biblica, Inc. TM. Used by permission. All rights reserved worldwide.

ISBN: 978-1-6642-7600-0 (sc)
ISBN: 978-1-6642-7599-7 (e)

Print information available on the last page.

WestBow Press rev. date: 09/09/2022

Dressing Up Death takes a simplistic everyday example, such as wearing clothes, and provides a tangible parallel metaphoric portrait of how grief is all about life.

John 11:25 "I am the resurrection and the life. He who believes in me will live, even though he dies;" (NIV)

To: Hannah Banana

To: Sherry

To: Leigh Anne

To: Kay, Ann, Lisa, Ginny, Dana,
Louise, Kathy, Shirley C.,
Quincy, and all the
family crew
Mom, Cynthia, Chip, Edy, Gibbons, Shep, and Ral
I love all of you very much.
Thank you beyond words.
and the Westbow staff. especially
Georgette thanks for sifting through all those emails!

Overview

Dressing Up Death (God's Unbecoming Fit of Grief)) is a ten chapter non-fiction book, divided into two parts, that takes a simple everyday example readers can relate to, such as wearing clothes, and provides a tangible parallel metaphoric portrait of how death is all about life. By taking the ultimate person, God the Father, and His view on death through the example of the death of Jesus, as well as other Biblical characters, readers will find **Dressing Up Death** a vivid book where penetrating questions, not pat answers, serve as much needed refuges for those who have traveled grief's rocky terrain.

Dressing Up Death is unique in that it addresses the parallel concept that death is not only abnormal for humans, but also for God Himself. **Dressing Up Death** openly invites those who have lost loved ones the freedom to rage against God as they encounter part one, **Sizing Up Death.** Part two, **Wearing Grief and Life,** allows readers to 'try on' what God ultimately created us to wear. Life. Healing comes from not dressing up death, but rather from the honest and intimate comparison that we, as humans, not deny the nature of who God created us to be; life givers and receivers. It is the goal of this book to have readers come away feeling overwhelmingly normal that their emotions towards death, an abnormal event, do indeed reflect the very essence and heart of God Himself.

About the Author

Debbie Vanderslice graduated with honors in history (B.A.) from Southern Methodist University in Dallas, Texas, where she played tennis on a full scholarship and was selected to the GTE Academic All Southwest Conference Honor team. With her strong writing skills and love for God, the Arkansas-bred-razorback has gone on to work with such Christian companies as DaySpring Cards and Celebration as a freelance writer. In addition to her published work with these companies, Debbie has had *Shameless*, a women's in-depth bible study published by New Hope Press. As well as *Gilead Now* by Westbow Press, and *Behind The Curtain*, and *The Addiction of the Dance* by Tate Publishers Debbie is a reality based mother, daughter, sister, and friend who knows the pain of grief. In 1997 Debbie lost her close friend and prayer partner to cancer. Martha ran her first marathon while pregnant with her second child and unknowingly had lymphoma cancer. Martha then endured six months of chemotherapy while pregnant and gave birth to a 100% healthy baby girl. In 1999 Debbie ran her first running race, a marathon, in memory of Martha.

Part I
Sizing Up Death

Chapter 1 Going Shopping

This opening chapter focuses on specifically how the death, and thus grief, took place for the reader. Using the realistic metaphor of dress, the reader can then relate to the underlying theme throughout the entire book of the abnormality of death not fitting. Whether the death was sudden, such as an accident, or slow, as in a terminal disease, the reader will see that no one chooses the outfit of grief.

Chapter 2 The Dressing Room

This chapter highlights the emotions and the tug-of-war feelings that come with death and grief. From denial to acceptance, and all the emotions therein, the reader will find comfort and hope that he/she is not alone as the author zeroes in on how we try out best to fit into grief somehow. It is in the dressing room we first dress up death in order to accommodate the reality that we actually live in a fallen world that indeed fits like a glove with our fallen human nature.

Chapter 3 The Purchase

This chapter brings to the forefront how we 'sell out' and accept that death is just a normal part of life. We tell ourselves that death is no big deal. Thus, we purchase the fit that God Himself never designed for us, or Him, to wear. By tracing the origin of why death is abnormal, the Garden of Eden, the reader will get his/her first glimpse at what was sold to Adam and Eve through Satan's deception: death. By comparing and contrasting the reader's own account of grief to the lie in the Garden, the reader will view a God who never intended any of his children taste the abnormality of death. Readers will find this chapter a refuge as the author gives personal examples of how she too made the purchase only to find herself in deeper pain and suffering.

Chapter 4 Taking Home the Outfit

Once we have bought into the lie that death is normal, we then take the outfit home to wear. On the way home, however, we find ourselves denying the very person God created us to be; life givers and receivers. As if something were indeed rotten in Denmark, or deep within our souls, the reader begins to feel uneasy with the whole aspect of death.

Chapter 5 The Tell-Tale Mirror

This chapter brings to the end the first part of the book, *Sizing up Death,* by looking at what lies deep within those who have buried family members, friend, and loved ones under the best of circumstances or the worst of situations: that death is radically abnormal. Try as we might, death is the most abnormal experience we have ever known intimately. This chapter bridges readers into part two of the book, *Wearing Grief and Life,* and begins to expose the tell tale mirror of why death is abnormal Biblically.

Part II
Wearing Grief and Life

Chapter 6 First Time Out

This chapter focuses on the disciples and how they too tried to wear grief in relation to Jesus about as well as the reader tries to wear his/her current loss. While the disciples told themselves they would go back to their normal lives before being chosen by God, they could no more dress up death better than the reader does today. Although we may laugh at the disciples attempt into seclusion of having never been affected by God, we too wear grief out for the first time in public about like they did of yester year. It didn't fit back then and it still doesn't today. By drawing a parallel between the disciples and the reader's own personal loss, the reader will find comfort in that he/she is not alone in the uncomfortable outfit of grief.

Chapter 7 The Dilemma of Death

After coming to terms that death is abnormal, the reader will then delve into the reality of why grief is so difficult to wear in terms of personal application. By engaging the reader to intimately and honestly ponder his/her own feelings associated with the loss, this chapter sets up the theme of the book and God's perspective Biblically on death and grief.

Chapter 8 A View from the Throne...or Floor

Readers will find this chapter their favorite, as they are comforted like nothing else. That is because God does the holding. The author uses the argument that while there is a "time to be born and a time to die," (Ecclesiastes 1:2) the real question posed in this book is whether or not God, the Daddy on the throne, thinks death is normal or not as He watched His only Son be murdered on a piece of wood that fateful Friday. Grief was no more 'normal' and 'fit' for God Himself that day than it is for us today. Thus, by Biblically using God as the author of death being abnormal, the reader finds a refuge like none other as he/she watches the Daddy on His knees and on heaven's floor wailing for His nail pierced Son. This chapter focuses on how the reader's own feelings regarding death and grief are in essence the very nature and heart of God Himself.

Chapter 9 Getting Real and Smelling Great

This chapter incorporates Mary of Bethany who anointed Jesus with perfume before His death. Does God understand the pain we are feeling and the utter helplessness of grief? Without a doubt God does and this chapter serves as a visual and moving example of how God sees into the hearts of those whose pain is so overwhelming that only truly He can fathom their heartfelt actions that the world dismisses. This chapter also links the theme of the final and culminating chapter and what captivates the Savior's heart like nothing else: love.

Chapter 10 Wearing Him

This final chapter leaves the reader pondering what is so abnormal about death and more specifically why. This chapter engraves on the readers hearts that death is about life. Thus, readers will walk away having given God their rage, pain, suffering, as well as asking who He created us to be; life givers and receivers. This closing chapter highlights the reader's own personal journey with grief not by ignoring or dressing up death, but rather by exploring with all honesty the search of why God Himself experienced the abnormalcy of death. The reader closes this chapter and book with a sense of not answers but rather questions, that serve as a mere backdrop into God and the quest of what He longs for all of us to wear. What was stolen publically in the Garden so long ago would one day be bought publically by the blood of Jesus. The Garden was just a glimpse to the finality of the cross.

Satan's perceived plan of defeat through death would allow each reader the freedom to step into what ultimately fits. Him. Life. Love.

Part 1

SIZING UP DEATH

Chapter 1

Going Shopping

Job 26:6 "Death is naked before God."

For the life of me I turned and swayed in every position imaginable. I pulled, shrugged, tucked, sucked in, sucked out, and finally gave up in utter disgust. What I once thought was a perfect fit, now hung loosely off me like a mocking clown's costume at the annual county fair. Try as I might, death was abnormal and grief the evil twin brother that wrapped his bony fingers around my neck like a scarf out of control.

Perhaps you too have unsuccessfully tried on grief. Maybe in your pain you also have tried to dress up death somehow. Just maybe you have tried to slip into the unflattering outfit of grief. None of us ask for it but it comes nonetheless. Death is an uninvited guest who many times rudely has us think him a 'normal part of life.'

However, I find death a difficult outfit to wear. Even for God Himself. If death were normal, then God Himself would never have allowed His only Son to be murdered before heaven's eyes when He had the power to stop the insaneness. In that unfathomable six hours called The Cross, God the Father wailed as He watched the most abnormal event of all time. Jesus Christ, God Incarnate, His only Son, dying at the hands of mere mortals.

Christ, once surrounded in perfection above, was now spread eagle, naked and dead below on a piece of timber. The Creator nailed to His own creation. Death normal? Not for heaven's sake that day it wasn't. Nor for us today.

I believe that as humans we dress up death. We try and tell ourselves it's not so bad. That death is a normal part of life, like a flower, that must succumb to winter. Many times we are told, "to everything there is a season." (Ecclesiastes 3:1, NIV) I am not debating or arguing that everything must be born and die. (verse 2) I can accept that fact of scripture. I pose the question, rather, if death is 'normal' or not from God perspective.

I believe death is an unbecoming and ultimately foreign fit that was never really intended for us to wear. Or for God. The Creator has and always will be into life. Even in death Jesus came to give back what was stolen in the Garden of Eden so long ago. Life.

This is not a book about how to handle grief. On the contrary. This book is for anyone who despises death. Who wails and wonders in their far corner of heaven if anyone understands. It is for anyone who has tried to buy into the prevailing Christian theory shoved down their throats, still drenched with salty and suffocating tears, that death is normal. This book is for all those who shake their fists at God, and tell Him they hate what He has allowed to happen. It is not a book for those who will walk through grief with no questions asked... It is a book quite simply for those who cannot be robots of faith as they grapple with the abnormalcy of death. This book is for all those who are tired of dressing up and accepting that death is just a normal part of life. This book is for those who gag, with rage in their hearts and love in their souls, on death, not life. This book is for those who long to strip down once and for all and step out of something that never fit anyway and look dreadfully drab to the core of their being.

I make no qualms that I am no expert educationally on death. I have no seminary degrees, which therefore qualify me to expound my theory of death being abnormal for God and for us, His creation. I have only God's perfect Word and my personal, intimate, and painful experiences as I have lost those I loved. An open, or sometimes closed casket, or alas, memorials, with only pictures surrounding me, have served as my reality based theory.

Come with me and embrace the very One who created us for life, not death. Journey with me as we come face to face with a real God who does not expect us to ignore the very nature of who He created us to be; life givers and receivers. Come with me as we go grave robbing and put on the intangibles and yet real clothes God intended for us to wear. Life. Come with me as we dress ourselves in Him and discover the perfect fit. Come with me as we give God our fury and honesty in the midst of retreating to our far corners of heaven to catch a glimpse of a broken hearted Father crying out to humanity how much He loves us. Come with me as we find hope and comfort in the midst of a long night called grief. There is only one rule for the trip: no clothes allowed. Only your pain, weeping, and suffering are allowed in this intimate quest of what we shall wear as our feeble faces reflect the mirror image of a God who knew death would never fit anyone.

One of the most precious verses to me is found in 2 Corinthians 1:3. It says that God is the "God of all comfort." Not some of comfort, but the God of all comfort. When my close friend died at the age of 30, I was inconsolable Tears flowed unceasingly. Grief reigned supreme. I have no doubt that when I say my world went 'gray,' you know exactly what I mean. Slow-motion feelings. Numbness. Shock. Denial. It was not until I stepped out and *embraced* the grief that the healing process took root. Bear in mind, it took two years and one marathon race later, for me to see the color in the world again. To smile. To laugh. To live again.

I have a theory. It is a Biblical theme throughout our lives as believers. It has to do with clothes. Are you ready for a shopping trip? Let's go back to the very beginning of time shall we. The Garden of Eden. Adam and Eve were created in perfection. The Garden of Eden was a perfect location with perfect relationships. If you will remember, Adam and Eve were naked and felt no shame. No clothes. No sin. No problem. It wasn't until after they sinned that they covered themselves. Genesis 3:7 says, "Then the eyes of both of them were opened, and they realized they were naked, so they sewed fig leaves together and made coverings for themselves." Sin doesn't just lie dormant in a sea of inactivity. It creeps and crawls and eventually walks and talks and before we know it, we are in the throngs of the consequences of sin.

God, if you will remember, made coverings for them with animal skins. The killing of a sacrificial animal was necessary and here we see the first example of the shedding of blood for the 'covering' of sins. Genesis 3:21 says, "The Lord God made garments of skin for Adam and his wife and clothed them." Is it not then, thematic in the Bible that sin, once entered into the human race, now stood at the door of salvation, and demanded coverings for us?

As we scurry around in life, much like roaches caught off guard when the lights are turned on, we must remember what the original plan was about. Life. Death only entered the human race when Adam and Eve winked at sin. Death, was never intended for us. Why did God vacate heaven? Because of the abnormalcy of death-a foreign and ultimately debilitating reality that beckons each one of us from our mother's womb.

Where is life found? It is found in the blood. Hebrews 9:22 says, "without the shedding of blood there is no forgiveness." That is, life is dependent on a beating heart. Is it not ironic that we find life in the blood of Jesus as He was dying? It is interesting and humbling to have a Savior who dies and gives His blood as a sacrifice for our lives.

I do not believe that it was a coincidence that Christ hung naked before all to see at the cross. The sinless life of Christ covered us because of His nakedness. "He who had no sin became sin for us." (2 Corinthians 5:21)

Thus, it all started in the Garden and ended at the cross. The Garden was just a glimpse to the finality of the cross. An interesting and key element is missing in the role of salvation-we are nowhere to be found. We do nothing but sin. We are absent when salvation took place in the Garden and at the cross. We cannot do anything. In fact, it is when we try to 'cover up' our sin that we make dreadful coverings for ourselves.

What does all this have to do with grief as we struggle on in this life without our loved one? Everything. We "are naked before God. (Job 26:6) Death is 'naked' before God, as are we, with all our feelings, emotions, pain and confusion. Nothing is hidden before an all knowing and compassionate God.

Perhaps you too are a little like me. Sometimes the stark reality of the world we live in comes closing in on me before I've had my two mugs of coffee. A senseless murder. An unfortunate accident. A horrible abuse. It is in this hour of need I cannot explain anything, yet unwillingly, sometimes grudgingly try to accept everything. I thirst for the understanding of God and the peace that only He can bring. The world does not offer such a luxury to my life.

It is undeniable. We live in a harsh world where people are constantly hurt by life's game of growing up. However, there is a softness and comfort in understanding God's unchanging character in the midst of our unstable and temporary world.

The purpose in writing this book is that we will be uplifted by the fact that we are not alone. So, whether you are like me and need an iv. of coffee in your arm to start the day, or you actually spring out of bed and eyes fully opened with a love for the world, **Dressing Up Death** is meant to make you feel overwhelmingly normal about grief, and at the same time, not deny the abnormalcy about death.

Chapter 2

The Dressing Room

*2 Corinthians 5:2, 4b "Meanwhile we groan, longing
to be clothed with our heavenly dwelling...so that
what is mortal may be swallowed up by life."*

I gazed lazily across the purple and pink splashed sky with relative
ease and serenity for a moment. Out among the Texas wild
flowers were children of all ages, as well as gigglish-tickled parents,
running to and fro in knee deep Indian paintbrushes and blooming
bluebonnets.

The children, oblivious to the itchy predicament their uncovered
legs were in, hurried feverishly in search of the hidden Easter eggs that
almost seemed to beckon their names. Time stood still for me in that
moment when Dusk called home his companions, Sun and Shadow.

Carrie sauntered down a hill as she helped her daughter find
egg filled delights buried deep within the grass. Carrie, stylish in
Martha's straw-brimmed hat with blue border, seemed to perfectly
play the role of fashionable friend.

Shalene, ever the domestic wonder queen, had decorated each
room in her new home by wrapping the walls with love and peace —
especially Martha's room of life. Shalene oozed the role of mother
and caretaker.

I, on the other hand, was dressed to kill in Martha's bright yellow,
round, smiley face underwear and bra that I wore underneath my
jeans and t-shirt. My goal, as always, was to be the incognito friend.

It was on this Easter weekend that I came to a startling and unsettling conclusion. It was a no denying reality that all three of us were trying our best to somehow dress up death. Martha's death.

Somewhere in the uncompromising recesses of our souls and spirits, as well as our mentalities, we were trying to fit into the unbecoming outfit of grief. We all hated wearing death. Death's bony fingers seemed to seal away something we all head dear. Life.

Shalene had her room of Martha. Carrie had Martha's hat. And, I wore Martha's smiley face undies and bra. Simply put, we were in our own separate ways trying to dress up what did not fit any of us. Call us insane, or just call us friends of Martha, either way we were desperately trying to deny Martha's death by holding onto her life and memory, be it a hat, picture, or bra.

However, there was one minor flaw to our unspoken theory. Martha wasn't coming back no matter how hard we tried to fit unto death's unbecoming wear.

I believe most people have accepted that death is a normal part of life. Grieving is normal. The feelings are 100% normal. However, death is abnormal. Again, I am not arguing whether or not death happens, because it does, but rather if death is abnormal or not.

Let's go shopping shall we? I hate to shop. I'd rather have a root canal compared to a trek to the mall.

Imagine with me if you will, that you decide to go shopping. Everything is going smoothly until a person grabs you from your refuge, or dressing area, and forces you to wear an outfit that is not suitable for you. The outfit doesn't fit. You really hate the outfit that the saleslady has picked out for you. The saleslady, Helga, then goes on to tell you that it is the only outfit you will be given. Your selections are then discarded by her. She then tells you that you will not be allowed to wear anything else but this one outfit she has thrust upon you. This particular and peculiar saleslady then tells you that you cannot buy anything else in the store or even the mall. You are not even allowed to wear the clothes you came to the mall in.

Of course, I am being silly aren't I? But hold on and go shopping with me for just a while longer. Death can be compared to an outfit. Helga stunned you and you are speechless. You have no options at all. Does that sound familiar to you? Did you get a call in the middle of the night? A doctor's grim diagnosis? An accident? Whatever road you must face with grief, you decide to give back to Helga and that gag awful outfit called death. However, there is one little problem. You are stark naked and Helga holds the one outfit deemed appropriate to wear. Thus, you accept and try on what you hate in terms of grief. Is it hitting home yet? It is a shopping trip God knows too well. Remember, He lost His only Son.

This leaves us with a dilemma. We either go naked or try on grief. We either go naked or try on grief. I am suggesting something that many churches are uncomfortable with. Go naked with your emotions and feelings with grief. Go ahead and hate death and mourn.

I have often wondered about our culture in terms of grief. We generally cry at funerals and occasionally in other grief stricken environments. However, if we watch the evening national news, we more than likely will see men and women of Eastern bloc countries in Europe, or Middle Eastern countries, crying uncontrollably. It is as if they are putting their whole being into it. It is an odd and difficult thing to watch; a broken and mourning heart.

Let me paint a story for you. I'm sure it is one you've already heard before. Lazarus, one of Jesus' best friends, has died. Jesus, who is relatively nearby, stays away on purpose. It was customary to bury a person on the third day. Jesus waited an extra day. Some scholars say He did this so that after He raised Lazarus from the dead, that there would be no dispute of whether Lazarus was actually dead or not. John 11:14 says, "So then he told them plainly, 'Lazarus is dead, and for your sake I am glad I was not there, so that you may believe. But let us go to him.'"

Notice what Christ does when He sees Lazarus' grave. It is the shortest verse in all the Bible. "Jesus wept." (John 11:35 NIV) The Greek word here for wept means wailing with great emotion...just like we see on the evening news. Could it be that the shortest verse in all of Scripture demonstrates God's own humanness? While we may remember Jesus raising Lazarus from the dead, we shouldn't forget the biggest miracle of all; God Incarnate, mourning a friend with unashamed friendship tears to weep. This reminds me of a poem I wrote after my friend, Martha died.

The Friendship Tears

I come to you with
unashamed friendship tears to weep.
You never tell me to stem them,
only to pour them at your feet.

She was a light down here
for just a short while.
I never dreamed the race she would run
on behalf of Heaven's mile.

Tenderness, touch, and trust
were ours indeed to share.
You freed my soul to love
as it was brokenly laid bare.

Many years ago I asked you
what friendship was all about.
You opened Heaven's graceful gate
and whispered Martha's name with evidence of a shout.

So deaf did I become
as I begged for time to keep.
"This my precious child is proof of my love for you,
because I have given you freedom with friendship tears to weep.
(DV Shameless, New Hope Publishers, 1998)

Have you ever gone shopping and loved an outfit so much that you buy it even when it didn't fit? Personally, I have succumbed to this dilemma and told myself, "All I have to do is lose five pounds and then I'll be able to get into it." Sound familiar? Will we fit into that outfit of death? Will we fit into the outfit of death somehow, even though it doesn't fit, or will we embrace the death of our loved one as Jesus did towards Lazarus? The decision is ours alone to make. No one can do it for us.

The overwhelming feeling I felt after Martha died was a sense of helplessness, much like I felt when she had been alive. I guess you could say I felt the entire ordeal was out of control. My control. I prayed for her healing. It didn't come. I prayed for the rapture. It didn't come. Finally, I prayed for her not to suffer anymore. And then she was gone. Amid hundreds and thousands of people praying for her, Martha left. And how it hurt. Have you been there friend? A cancer? An accident? A surgery?

In her dying days in the hospital, I was horrified and yet drawn to what I saw. Just like a moth drawn to a flame, so too was I drawn to Martha. While her body and mind failed, her spirit rose to heights I'd never witnessed before. I saw first hand what Paul refers to as a drink offering. Philippians 2:17 says, "But even if I am being poured out like a drink offering on the sacrifice and service coming from your faith, I am glad and rejoice with all of you." It was both disturbing and addicting at the same time. What was it, in the midst of suffering and death, that I found so illuminating? It was a *life* in all its mystery and splendor. I saw life in the purest form. That of Jesus Christ. It reminds me of another poem I wrote as Martha was dying right before my eyes.

Bed of Pain

Isaiah 42:3 "My tears have been my
food day and night." (NIV)

Lie down upon this bed of pain.
The sorrows deep you can't contain.
I come gently to tuck you in
and hold you close from evil's den.
Though your hurt is a well dug deep
I'll soften your pillow so you will sleep.
The bliss of peace will overflow
my healing love you will know.
Sleep well with this longing of mine.
For I'm The Bliss you will find.
(DV Shameless Bed of Pain, 1998)
Psalm 38:9 "All my longings lie open
before you O Lord." (NIV)

Do you ever wonder if God sees and hears out pain? He does. Remember, He is the God of *all* comfort. Won't you bring Him all your grief today? Go ahead, lie down on your bed of pain. I think your be surprised how empathetic He will be. He's been where you are. Take a chance on giving Him your grief. I did, and it has made all the difference in the world. He is The Bliss we will find in the midst of death.

Chapter 3

The Purchase

"There is something about the whole process of death
that seems so wrong to me. It suddenly became clear to
me that this was never God's plan" 'Shelia Walsh
(*Living Fearlessly*)

"In the blink of an eye. In the snap of a finger. In the beat of a heart. It happened so quickly she wasn't sure what to think. Or say. Or do. Silently the lie had crawled up to her and before reality had time to sink in, she had slept in his bed. A dream she thought it would be. Rather the charmed slumber turned out to be her worst nightmare. She had been promised and gone to sleep with the keys to the world, but awoke with merely the chains to hell. That promise beside her turned out to be a lie from the chief of all liars.

She went to sleep a queen in the garden of perfection and woke up a pauper in the prison of all cells. The charmer turned out to be a snake. The promise a lie. The tainted keys that once held the world at her beck and call now held her captive to her own personal prison. Silently it happened. Quickly it was stolen. It would take God Himself venturing this earth for Eve and Adam, and consequently all mankind, in order to beat Satan at his own game.

"Eve tried to hide it. She ran from it. She even tried to cover it up. Literally. Where there was once perfection, there was now only shame. Imperfection was the game and it was now a part of Eve.

Hide it. Cover it. Lie about it. The game of sine, shame, and death had begun. What Satan stole secretly in the Garden of Eden would one day have to be brought back publically by the blood of Jesus. The Garden was just a glimpse to the finality of the cross.

Eve didn't merely tremble when she heard God walking in the Garden at dusk that fateful day. She was physically, emotionally, and spiritually terrified to the point of never wanting to see her Creator face to face again. So, when God asked her what she'd done, Eve lowered her shame-ridden, darting eyes and gave what she'd never given before. An excuse as well as a lie. "The serpent deceived me, and I ate." (Genesis 3:13b, ESV)

It wasn't a total lie. Satan had deceived her. Eve immediately despised not only herself, but also what she had done and especially what she was now doing; covering by the bushes in the darkness of sin and shame instead of walking in the light of the truth with her Creator hand and hand through the Garden.

Eve thoughtlessly in a second traded who God had perfectly created and intended her to be and bought the ultimate lie of all time-that she was defected to her very core in some way even though she was in a perfect relationship with God. The game of sin, shame and death had begun secretively in the Garden and hiding, darkness and death were the players who presented themselves. It would take God's own Son being crucified publically to bring back truth, light and life to all who would venture down Satan's unending road." (Shameless, Debbie Vanderslice. p.32,33)

Because of Adam and Eve, all of us must do battle with death. Genesis 2:16-17 "you are free to eat from any tree in the garden; but you must not eat from the tree of the knowledge of good and evil, for when you eat of it you will surely die."(ESV Shameless, Debbie Vanderslice 1998)

Had Adam and Eve obeyed God, then death would be a moot issue. Once sin entered the human race, then the battle lines for death and life would be drawn. Jesus, God Incarnate, came to earth as a human to bridge the gap that separated us from Him due to the disobedience in the Garden. It was not until Jesus died and rose again that we would and could experience life in all its' beauty.

Now that you've met Helga, the saleslady, let's take our outfit of death to the dressing room. Helga, if you will remember is the saleslady at the store in which you are shopping. Your mind and heart cannot make sense of what Helga is telling you. The only outfit you are allowed to wear is the one she is providing you with. You cannot even wear your own clothes home.

Once inside the small dressing room Helga bangs on the door and says to hurry up. You timidly tell her you are having trouble with the outfit. Helga just laughs and tells you that it will fit. There is no other alternative. Once on, it looks awful and doesn't fit and you begin to cry. Helga makes you model it around the store. She proudly announces to the other shoppers that you look stunning. The other shoppers echo the compliments that Helga has bestowed upon you.

After many difficult moments you decide that you are trapped. First of all, you cannot go around naked. You are forced into this unbecoming outfit to wear. Secondly, it doesn't really fit but you decide that it will eventually fit better at home. Thus, you tell yourself that you must buy this outfit or else be ostracized from everyone . You hate that you have no choice or say in the matter.

Does this sound familiar to you, friend? You and I were not given the opportunity to pass on death via a loved one. Death wrapped his bony fingers around us and we never got a chance to unleash him. Whatever way your loved one died, we can be sure of this: Helga came to use and forced us to wear what God never intended for any of us to wear: death.

We were created to be life givers and receivers. Remember that Adam and Eve experienced life beyond measure; a life in perfection free from the tarnish of sin and death. Up until that dark moment when Eve ate of the fruit, death was nowhere to be found. However, once Eve disobeyed and sinned, death was a happening reality for the rest of mankind. I wonder if Eve felt what all of us feel at the moment we lose someone vital to us. Numb. Did Eve feel shocked at what happened? When my friend Martha died, I felt numb. Disbelief at death. Eve, once surrounded in perfection, was now knee deep in sin and death.

How odd that God had to send His Son into the world to redeem it. Christ, in heaven, had everything. Why, can you imagine the insaneness of choosing to leave perfection and all those angels bowing down saying holy, holy, holy.

It was never God's intention that death be a 'part' of life. He never willed that for our lives. Does death happen? Yes. All of us will taste of death. But it was never God's plan for us. I agree with Shelia Walsh in her book, *Living Fearlessly* She says we got "Plan B." In getting Plan B we are faced with the reality of being fallen human creatures. We are born into sin and in "death" as we carry on in this life.

Thus, it is in the dressing room of the world that we buy into the lie that because death happens to everyone it is therefore normal. Nothing could be further from the truth. If death were normal then Jesus would have never left heaven. It is because death is so abnormal that He left perfection in order to save us from sin and death.

But, notice that the world tells us that death is normal. After all, death will visit everyone. Even in the church today, many grief stricken believers are unfortunately forced to fit into the outfit of death as it relates to faith. That is to say, many Christians must put on a happy face in grief in order to save face on their loss because their faith is on display. In other words, we should not question God, His motives, or the loss we feel because we will be viewed as weak and/or an immature believer.

The feelings we go through with grief are normal. Shock, denial, anger, etc. But have you ever wondered what would have happened if Eve would have never eaten the apple? Sin and death would have never entered the human race. Christ would never have visit earth and we'd still be living in perfection. Ah, it sounds ideal doesn't it? But, unfortunately, reality prevails. Our feelings associated with grief are normal because of what happened in the Garden. But the fact that God Almighty, Christ, had to come down to earth as a human is not normal. Thus, death is perhaps the oddest reality of all. God becomes man in order to save us from what He never intended. Death.

As humans we masterfully try to squeeze into what does not fit us. It is in the dressing room of life that we deny who God created us to be and slip into what has never fit since the beginning of time. And so, we decide as fallen humans that Helga is right. It fits, kind of. The other alternative is just too scary. We decide that nakedness is not too widely accepted by the church. So, we leave the dressing room convinced that death will somehow fit better as we leave for home.

Many times in the church we are faced, almost shamed, into putting on a brave face and telling everyone that our loved one who died, is in fact, in heaven. In a better place. No more suffering. Finally at rest from this cruel, harsh world. We try to convince ourselves that "all things work together for good." (Romans 8:28) But, underneath, back in the recesses of our minds, we despise and abhor the fact that we will not see, hear, or talk to our loved one on a daily basis. We will have to wait until we die. That depresses us even more.

I miss the little things about Martha. I miss her voice. Her smile. And yes, I miss her grilled cheese sandwiches on her homemade bread. I miss our prayer time together. I guess when you get down to it, I miss her. Her life.

I believe that the days and weeks that follow a loved one's death is crucial to how we will respond spiritually. I chose the purchase of death and put on a happy face. I gave all the accepted answers that the church loves to hear, yet my grief only lasted longer due to my inauthenticity. Finally, I just got naked with grief. I wept uncontrollably. I wept bitterly for Martha. And then something miraculously happened. I started 'celebrating' Martha's life. I went naked with my emotions spiritually. I slurped our slurpees. I ate our grilled cheese sandwiches on homemade bread. I ate our tootsie pops. I ran our marathon, and I celebrated Martha with her mother.

While I celebrated Martha's life, many people began to question my quest. My family and friends told me to 'move on.' Yet, what they didn't realize was that I was moving on...in my own time and way. Ecclessiates doesn't specify how long to mourn, only that there is a time to mourn. Instead of letting the church dictate my behavior and grieving, I let God do the directing.

Are you overwhelmed with your grief? That's ok, remember Jesus was too at the death of his good friend, Lazarus. Go ahead, weep and wail. Get overwhelmed. It is the very reason God came to earth as a human and endured great shame...to give us *life* in the midst of grief. Celebrate your loved one. Get vocal about it. After all, we have the perfect example of how much a death can hurt. But ponder this: death didn't stop Christ from living the life He was called to. Yes, mourn deeply. Love generously. And Live expectantly. Expect great things. Life is just around the corner.

Chapter 4

Taking Home the Outfit

1John 3:14a "We know that we have passed
out of death into life..." (ESV)

Once we have bought into the lie that death is normal, we then take the outfit home to wear. On the way home, however, we find ourselves denying the very person God created us to be; life givers and receivers. As if something were indeed rotten in Denmark, or deep within our souls, we begin to feel uneasy with the whole aspect of death.

I can think of no better an example than Christ. He wore the robe of human being and think of all the things he had to endure or suffer through. He had to fight hunger. He was thirsty. He had to fight his urges for the opposite sex. Hold on. Hold on Deb. God is sexual? Well, scripture tells us he was tempted in *every* way and was without sin. Hmm. I know it sounds so human to have sexual temptations. But look at what Luke says, "And Jesus, full of the Holy Spirit, returned from the Jordan and was led by the Spirit in the wilderness for forty days, being tempted by the devil (Luke 4:1,3 ESV) So temptation is all Satan. Jesus was tempted by Satan, not God. God is not the author of temptation. Satan is. Sometimes in grief we get lost. We don't know who to turn to. Will they tell us to get over it? Your faith is on trial. You will be judged on how you react to death. But God is into life .He does not judge us as to how long we mourn. He is right there morning with us. No matter how long we stay on the floor wailing in the muck and mire. He's there .Never will leave us no matter what. He is on the floor with us.

See if you can relate to this poem I wrote after my prayer partner died.

Somewhere

Somewhere along the path I lost my way.
Somewhere along the way I lost my hope.
Somehow without my hope I found resentment.
Somehow my resentment turned to anger.
Somehow my anger grew into bitterness.
Somehow my bitterness flew into rage.
Somehow my rage consumed me.
Somewhere in the rage I blamed you, O God .
For all the pain.
For all the abandonment.
For all the fear
For all the sorrow.
For all the grief. For all the tears.
For all the dreams never lived
For all the hopes left unfulfilled.
Do you know O God, how difficult this is for me?
To take your hand and trust you pin what I cannot see.
You know my past and pain so well,
For it is real to me.
Can you take my tattered life \
and help me live for eternity?
Somewhere along the road, O Lord,
I gave my heart \
Somewhere along the trodden path
I lost those that I loved.
If I give to you my honesty
And choose to do what is right,
Will you in turn give me the strength

to last the good and holy fight?
Because I come before you as a little child
So very very lost.
Somewhere along the way I blamed you
For all my pain and thus the cost.

Debbie Vanderslice
Shameless
New Hope Publishers
p.77
1998

"Way to go hot momma. Looking good. We have all been there. If you have lived on this earth, you have heard it all. They, being the general public, say you look awesome wearing death. They and you are "dressing up death." You cannot put your finger on it but you get the strange feeling that you must either succumb to their condolences or go naked. I am suggesting that you do the unfathomable thing. Go naked instead of trying to fit into that unbecoming fit of grief.

In 2 Corinthians 5:2-3 it says "For in this tent we groan, longing to put on our heavenly dwelling, if indeed by putting it on we may not be found naked." (ESV)

Our groaning is just a glimpse to the finality of the cross. Every bad thing that happens to us can be used by God for his glory. And I do mean everything. What basis do I have for this bold claim? Only God's perfect Word. Romans 8:28 says, "And we know that for those who love God all things work together for good, for those who are called according to his purpose." (ESV)

It doesn't say some things. It says **all** things work together for good....To me that means God can take the most dire situation with the most dire of people and turn it into His glory. Let's look at Paul, formerly known as Saul. He hated the Christians. Persecuted them relentlessly. And then God did his thing. It is called redemption. He chose the least likely of candidates to carry out his divine plan.

Quite simply He chose a murderer, slanderous, and Christ hater to spread His word. And boy did Saul, now called Paul live for Christ.

Paul was stoned, beaten, shipwrecked, whipped and eventually put to death because of his incredible devotion to Christ. Listen to his final words to us. Would he die for a lie that Jesus was not the Messiah? Absolutely not. Who would die for a lie? Not me. And not Paul. Here are some of Paul's last words.

"I have fought the good fight, I have finished the race, I have kept the faith. (2 Timothy 4:7, ESV)

When we take home the outfit of death it just doesn't fit. Maybe we are just plain old mad at God. Let's look at the 5 stages of grief by Kubler-Ross"

1. Denial
2. Anger
3. Bargaining
4. Depression
5. Acceptance

Where are you in the stages? I must have stayed in the anger phase for over 3 years. I did not talk to God at all. I had all my reasons why I was divorcing God, but instead of walking away I was flat out running from God.

I skipped over the bargaining phase and went into the depression stage. I stayed there for another 2-3 years. It has only been in the last year that I finally accepted Martha's death. But it took me a long time. Very long. Thank goodness that God grades on the curve. I was lost for so long.

Bed of Pain

"My tears have been my food day and night."(Shameless, ESV, p. 93)
Isaiah 42:3

Lay down upon this bed of pain.
The sorrows deep you can't contain.
I come gently to tuck you in
And hold you close from evil's den.
Though your hurt is a well dug deep
I'll soften your pillow so you will sleep.
The bliss of peace will overflow
My healing love you will know.
Sleep well with this longing of mine.
For I'm the bliss you will find.
Debbie Vanderslice

Here's another poem I wrote after Martha died. I found no solace except when I put it down on paper. See if this ministers to you.

My Road

Psalm 16:11
"You made known to me the path of life." (ESV)

I'm venturing down a road O Lord
That doesn't feel quite familiar.
I am unsure where it's leading
Yet that stops me not
It is a dangerous steep path'
and nothing is comfortable, O dear God.
I find myself unable to go back
Where predictability was my refuge. \
Something is beckoning me further on the road,
So addicting in its uncertainty.
Could it be, O sweet Jesus
That what draws me towards the darkness
Is the illumination of you? \
For in this blind walk of mine perhaps

I'm finally beginning to see who you
are and chose I really am.
(Shameless, New Hope Publishers, p.93)
Debbie Vanderslice

As you can tell, songs really minister to me. Sometimes in a way that mere words cannot. Once I have connected to a song it becomes part of my morning ritual. When I am doing my makeup and brushing my hair. I listen to the words I have fallen in love with and play it over and over. It becomes my mantra. One such song is a song about heaven. It is so well written I am still in awe of it. Read the lyrics below and see if it soothes your soul the way it does for me.

I Can Only Imagine

Written and Sung by Mercy Me
I can only imagine
what it will be like
When I walk by your side
I can only imagine
what my eyes will see
When your face is before me
I can only imagine
Yeah

Our bodies long to be clothed by Christ. We want nothing more than to take home our eternal home dressed in Him. He alone clothes us. Read the following verses. I can think of no better way to end this chapter.

John 10:11 "And the Lord God made for Adam and for his wife garments of skins and clothed them (ESV).

Job 11:10a "You clothed me with skin and flesh..." (ESV)

Notice our role. We do nothing but sin. God alone clothes us. He alone is the one who saves. Not us.

The Tell-Tale Mirror

1Corinthians 13:12a
"For now we see in a mirror dimly..."
(ESV)

This chapter brings to the end the first part of the book, Sizing up Death. By looking at what lies deep within those who have buried family members, friends and loved ones under the best circumstances or the worst of situations: that death is radically abnormal. Try as we might, death is the most abnormal experience we have ever known intimately. This chapter bridges readers into part two of the book, Wearing Grief and Life, and begins to expose the tell- tale mirror of why death is abnormal Biblically.

Michael Jackson Lyrics

"Man In The Mirror

I'm gonna make a change,
For once in my life
It's gonna feel real good,
Gonna make a difference
Gonna make it right...
As I, turn up the collar on my

Favorite winter coat
This wind is blowin'my mind
Can we make that change? Of course we can.
With God's help we can do anything!!

Part II

WEARING GRIEF AND LIFE

Chapter 6

First Time Out

Jeremiah 8:18
"My joy is gone; grief is upon me; my heart is sick within me."
(ESV)

This chapter focuses on the disciples and how they too tried to wear grief in relation to Jesus about as well as the reader tries to wear his/her current loss. While the disciples told themselves they would go back to their normal lives before being chosen by God, they could no more dress up death better than the reader does today. Although we may laugh at the disciples attempt into the seclusion of having never been affected by God, we too wear grief out for the first time in public about like they did of yester year. It didn't fit back then and it still doesn't today. By drawing a parallel between the disciples and the reader's own personal loss, the reader will find comfort in the fact that he/she is not alone in the uncomfortable outfit of grief.

The first time we wear the outfit of grief, we are very self conscious. Is everyone looking at us? What are they saying? Either they will give their unasked advice and therefore are of no good. Or they will simply hug us with no requests and to call if you need an ear. Those that have known death grief, intimately will just hug us. No strings attached. Wouldn't it be nice to have a big bear hug with no advice.Nothing is worse than to get advice from one of those super Christians who has all the answers.

Oh, you know the kind I am trying to convey. They say "praise

God, she/he is in a better place now. He/she is in glory. No more pain, only glory." You feel like knocking this unsympathetic person in the face. Let her/him go through what you are feeling and then let him/ her praise God till the cows come home. Instead of God saying I understand, He sent Christ to say *I know*. It is called empathy. That is one thing God did for us. He became human so to relate to all we go through in this life. An understanding Savior.

It wasn't until Christ came back to encourage the disciples that they then found the courage to carry out His mission and the role they would play in spreading the gospel. That was their destiny.

By now you know how much God ministers to me through music. I would not put it in this book unless it were so. Check out this song on destiny. Our destiny is found in The One who loves us. No matter what. Take a look.

Destiny
Lyrics and song by

Twila Paris
Buried in the heart of every child of His creation
Is a deep desire for which we seldom find the words
As each poet sings of searching for his own salvation
Once again the common drum is heard
Beating out the question
Only honest and courageous hearts will answer
Will answer
Do you know Him?
This is your destiny
Will you obey Him
There is an open door

Look at John 19:b "...the doors being locked where the disciples were." (ESV) The disciples were fearful to say the least. What had once been an open door gig was now a closed session with the doors being locked. Their good friend was now dead on a piece of timber. Who would be next? Did the authorities know where they were? What had they done the last few years with Christ? Simply put, they were petrified.

Need proof that the disciples were scared? Just take a look at Peter. Jesus told him that the rooster would crow three times that he would deny not even knowing Jesus. How's that for friendship?

Let's take a look at what God's perfect word has to say about this:'

Luke 22:60-61 ...man I do not know what you are talking about. And immediately, while he was still speaking, the rooster crowed. ...and he went out and wept bitterly."(ESV)

If you are doubtful about the whole Christ thing, think of this question. Would you die for a lie? Did you know that eleven of the twelve disciples were martyred. The only disciple to die of natural causes was John. They would not and did not die for a lie. Were they fearful at first? Without a doubt they were. They didn't merely shut the door after Christ was crucified. No they locked it. Would they be next? Yes, they were scared. And with good reason.

Jesus, Incarnate was nailed to a tree in about one minute. Who would be next. But let's not stop there. After all, we have Good News. That piece of timber didn't keep him down for long. No, He was sent to give us hope. Hope was not all about the death of our savior but it is found in his redeeming love. Even in death we are redeemed by His resurrection and coming back from death to give us life. He was dead and now is alive for you and me. Out of something painful comes God's saving grace. Out of death comes life.

What will we do with this information? We can do nothing. We can intellectually accept it. Or we can get down and dirty and not merely give Him lip service and say all the right things.

But we can put our faith to good use and good works. It takes trust. We may say we have it but look at the disciples. Out of 12 disciples11 died martyr's deaths. Only John was not murdered. Many think because God led him to write the end of the Bible.

Back to the 12. Would they die for a lie? I seriously doubt they thought "oh boy today I will be stone or crucified. No, they were devoted to The Truth and sharing the Gospel. Would you die for a lie? Their courage inspired the next generation and the next generation and so on. People across the board have died for the cause of Christ. Salvation maybe cheap but sanctification is not.

I would enter seclusion mode if I were the disciples. And they did. However, when God finds you and ministers to your lives will never be the same. Just ask doubting Thomas as he is commonly referred to. Take a look at this scripture:

"Eight days later, his disciples were inside again, and Thomas was with them. Although to you lives will never be the same. Just ask doubting Thomas as he is commonly referred to. Take a look at this scripture:

Then he said to Thomas "put your finger here, and see my hands; and put out your hand and place it in my side Do not disbelieve but believe." (John 20:27, ESV)

Belief and trust are two totally different things. If you believe you can swim you might or might not can. Trust is jumping in the pool and believing/trusting that dad will catch your two year old. Trusting is a lot harder than believing. Trusting is where the rubber meets the road. We can believe all day long but until there is action with it is not trusting. It takes a lot of courage to trust. This next song lyrics is by Twila Paris again. Maybe this song will help you see the difference between belief and trust. It sure helped me.

Do I Trust You
Lyrics and sung
By Twila Paris

Sometimes my little heart can't understand
What's in Your will what's in your plan
So many times I'm tempted to ask you why
But I can never forget it for long
Lord what You do could not be wrong
So I believe You even when I must cry
Chorus:
Do I trust You Lord does the robin sing

The Dilemma of Death

2Corinthians 2-3
*"For in this tent we groan, longing to put on our heavenly
dwelling, if indeed by putting it on we may not be found naked."*
(ESV)

After coming to terms that death is abnormal, we will then delve of why grief is so difficult to wear in terms of personal application. By engaging the reader to intimately and honestly ponder his/her feelings associated with the loss, this chapter sets up the theme of the book and God's perspective on death and grief.

Losing a loved one can have a decisive and difficult impact on surviving family and friends. When my friend, Martha, died at age 30, I felt as though the world went on but I remained in slow motion. I wrote this after she died. See if you can relate if you have lost a loved one.

The Refining
By Debbie Vanderslice

Shameless
New Hope Publishers

p.80

1Peter 1:7
"...so that the genuineness of your faith-more
precious than gold that perishes though it is tested
by fire-may be found to result in praise and glory
and honor at the revelation of Jesus Christ."
(ESV)

Sometimes this grief washes over me
Like the ocean waves crashing against the sand.
Unending. Ceaseless.Perpetual.
To the mere spectator turned vacationer
The water, brings with it peace, solitude, and rest.
But to the resident who beaches upon
Its shore day after day and month after month,
The waves carry pain, loneliness, and grief.
How long, O Lord,
Will the waters captivate my life?
My every move. Thought Response.
My world stopped while the world went rudely went on.
My tears flowed unceasingly while others
seemed to smile effortlessly
Where is my hope O God?
Why do these lips honestly confess the horrors of my heart?
For whatever if gone now
I can rest assured that
You are still in control,
And will one day reveal the seemingly painful
Madness of the here and now,
To the overwhelmingly speechless perfection
Of your divine plan.
Your method is perfect.
Your timing is perfect.
May this life of mine not tarry in vain
As I seek Your hand during this molding process.

Have you ever wondered why the obituaries say survivors?

What does it mean? I think simply put they are surviving all the flood of memories, some good some bad, and are surviving being without the deceased's family and friends .They are surviving all the things they use to do with the departed. It is a tragedy at any age of the dearly deceased. Death is a bad thing. But, we as Christians, have hope to see our loved one again. Heaven gives us hope for the future event.

We have an appointed time to be born and to die. Look at Ecclesiastes 3:1-2 "For everything there is a season, and a time for every matter under heave: a time to be born, and a time to die." (ESV)

A couple of years ago I cheated death. You can call it near death experience if you must. I call it a God thing. I had a stroke and my heart stopped for two minutes. One minute and then another minute. Call it what you like but I had no heart beat for 2 minutes. Before they shocked me back to life here was my dream.

I dreamed I was in a good place because I wasn't in any pain. I dreamed I was in heaven I think .I had on a white robe that came down to my shins. Martha was there and had on the same thing. She had a bouquet of flowers.

> I said, "You've got hair Martha."
> She replied, "but of course."
> I said, "where are you going with those flowers?"
> She said, 'To see the King of course."
> I said, 'I want to go too."
> Martha laughed," you can't, It is not your time yet."

And then she was gone. I will never forget that. I believe that was a near death experience because I heard the paramedics say, "she's back, we got a pulse."

This dream remains the most vivid dream I have ever had. I will never forget it. Do I believe in God. Yes. Do I believe in Christ. Yes. Did I have a near death experience. Yes. I have always been afraid of death. Not anymore. It was the most surreal thing I have ever experienced. Ever. Now I am living like I am dying. Hey that is a song. As you could ascertain by now music is a big part of my life and writing. Read the lyrics of this song.

Live Like You Were Dying Lyrics
By Tim McGraw

He said I was in my early forties
With a lot of life before me
When a moment came that sopped me on a dime

I spent most of the next days
Looking at the x-rays
Talking bout the options and
Talking bout sweet time

We should all live as we are dying. We are born and thus are dying. May we all seek God as we are dying every single day and, every single minute. That is the dilemma of death.

Chapter 8

A View from the Throne...or Floor

Isaiah 6:1b
"...I saw the Lord sitting upon a throne, high and lifted up; and the train of his robe filled the temple," (ESV)

Readers will find this chapter their favorite, as they are comforted like nothing else. That is because God does the holding. I will use the argument that while there is a time "to be born and a time to die," (Ecclesiastes 1:2, ESV) the real question posed in this book is whether or not God, the Daddy on the throne, thinks death is normal or not as He watched His only Son be murdered on a piece of wood that fateful; Friday. Grief was no more "normal" and "fit" for God Himself that day than it is for us today.

Thus, by Biblically using God as the author of death being abnormal, we will find a refuge like none other as he/she watches the Daddy on His knees and on heaven's floor wailing for His nail pierced Son. This chapter will focus on how the reader's own feelings regarding death and grief are in essence the very nature and heart of God Himself.

Every time we see The Father depicted in scripture He is on His throne. We never see Him off his throne. That to me means he is always in control. Of what you might ask? Of the whole world and its inhabitants and creatures. A sparrow doesn't fall out of his nest without the Father knowing it. Likewise, we, as humans, don't go through something of grave report without God the Father knowing about it. He is always depicted as being in total control. Who better to sing about God being in control than Twila Paris.

God is in Control Lyrics
By Twila Paris

This is no time for fear
This is the time for faith and dermination
Don't lose the vision here carried away by the motion
Hold on no all that you hide in your herat
There is one thing that has always been ture
It holds the world together
God is in control

God the father is never ever depicted in the Word as off his throne. He never gets off His throne. He is in complete control. Now isn't it amazing that God came into this filthy and unclean world to become human like we are in order to not merely whisper I know, but to shout I understand. He was not sympathizing but rather empathizing . Can you imagine the all you could eat buffet in heaven? Fahitas. Ice cream. Steak. You name it God gave it up for us. Now that's love. Real love.

If I were God, let me ponder that for a few moments, I would have never subjected myself to being a mere mortal. Being born to a teeny bopper, being told what to do as an adolescence,, hunger, no place to live, itinerant preacher. You know, human things, when he had the power to stop the insaneness. The cross. Now that's a good one. Allowing man to crucify Him. And for what? Ungrateful human beings.

Think of God being over all the universe. Nothing happens that he does not know about. Even the sparrow that falls out of the tree. All is worth His concern. Nothing is too big or too small. He loves us communicating with Him. We are his pride and joy.

Nothing brings Him more pleasure than us talking/praying to Him. It is why He ventured down here to earth as a human, Jesus, and endured death, death on a cross and let humans crucify Him when He had the power to stop the insaneness. Why? Because He loves us. Again I say why? His love for us is unfathomable. It is scary. But scary good.

What did God the Father think of His only Son venturing down to earth to die for the sins of mankind. Was there pleading to not go and leave him. No. Were there tears at the cross? Wailing because He had to carry His own cross and the blood stained head with the crown of thrones? What was it like to have been the truth yet treated as a lie? What was it like to have been the light of the world and yet to have been snuffed out by the world? O God, what was it like?

As I think back to my carefree days of life before kiddos, I wonder what I did with all that time? When children come they are a blessing. But, what did I do before kids came? Carefree is word that comes to mind. But oh, the blessings and love after that baby came "out of that shute." I have never had so much love pour forth at once. Happiness and tears of joy. Then came the toddler years. But we survived didn't we. Then school and first time friends.

Then Lord help us the teenage years. Next is the college years. Shock shock my daughter finally wants to spend time with me. This is the age she is at now. Early adulthood. Such a sweet sweet age. I wouldn't trade this time for anything. Anything. What is God trying to teach me. Sometimes I feel as though He is refining me. How has God refined you during your walk? I bet it has been an adventure.

Chapter 9

And The House Was Filled

John 12:3
"Mary therefore took a pound of expensive ointment made from pure nard, and anointed the feet of Jesus and wiped his feet with her hair. The house was filled with the fragrance of the perfume."
(ESV)

This chapter incorporates Mary of Bethany who anointed Jesus with perfume before His death. Does God understand? Without a doubt God does and this chapter serves as a visual and moving example of how God sees into the heart of those who pain is so overwhelming that only truly He can fathom their heartfelt action that the world dismisses .This chapter also links the theme of the final and culminating chapter and what captivates the savior's heart like nothing else: love

Jesus went to Bethany during His last days? Why there? I think it wasn't where but who was there. He went to Bethany to draw support from those he loved most and who loved him most.

Namely Mary, Martha, and Lazarus. These were his closest friends. Lazarus, a.k.a. the dead man walketh. And sweet Mary and Martha. You remember Martha the domestic queen. And Mary, I am going to sit and listen at our feet, never mind the dishes. Mary the listener, and Martha, the worried busy domestic queen. Why did He travel to Bethany? I think it was because he was getting strength for his upcoming events. The denial of a close friend (Peter), the beating beyond recognition, and the resurrection.

I don't know about you, but that is a full plate to have come your way. Lots of emotions. Lots of pain and suffering But oh, "...that my joy may be in you, and that your joy may be full."(John 15:11, ESV) .

Mary of Bethany is always depicted in Scripture as being at Jesus' feet. A position of respect and submissiveness. She wanted to learn whatever she could from Christ. She did not want to miss on word. While her sister is in the kitchen preparing the meal, Mary is intently listening to all Jesus had to say.

Let's talk about Mary. Let's see what scripture says

John 12:3-4 "Mary therefore took a pound of expensive ointment made from pure nard and anointed the feet of Jesus and wiped his feet with her hair. The house was filled with the fragrance of the perfume." (ESV)

First of all Mary gave from her heart. What could she do to communicate her love and devotion to Jesus? There was only one thing that was of value. The bottle of pure nard. It was worth over a year's wages. It was a desperate act of love. She didn't think about it for a long time, she just did it. She wanted her friend and Savior to smell great for his death. Yes, I believe she knew He was going to die. She wiped His feet with her hair. Again, this was a desperate and unplanned act of love. When true love is sacrificed it is a sweet aroma that engulfs all around.

Yet another Mary who sacrificed for the cause of heaven was none other than Mary the mother of Jesus. Think about her wild pregnancy. A virgin yet pregnant. Born in a stable. Yet she knew when he was in the temple debating with the scholars that he was special. At 33 an itinerant preacher. She knew at his birth that He was from God. Was He God? Did she really raise God Almighty? The following song lyrics minister to me. How about you?

Mary Did You Know
Lyrics by Mark Lowry

Mary did you know
That your baby boy will someday walk on water?
Mary did you know
That your baby boy will save our sons and daughters?
Did you know that your baby boy
Has come to make you new?
This child that you delivered will soon deliver you.

Wearing Him

Genesis 3:21
"And the Lord God made for Adam and for his wife garments of skins and clothed them"
(ESV)

This final chapter leaves you, the reader, pondering what is so abnormal about death and more specifically why. This chapter engraves on the readers hearts that death is about life. Thus,,readers will walk away having given god their rage, pain, and suffering we as asking who He created us to be; life givers and receivers. This closing chapter highlights the readers' own personal journey with grief not be ignoring or dressing up death, but rather by exploring with all honesty the search of why God Himself experienced the abnormalcy of death. The reader shoes this chapter and book with a sense of not answers but rather questions, that serve as a mere backdrop into God and the quest of what He longs for all of us to wear. What was stolen secretly in the Garden so long ago would one day be bought by publically by the blood of Jesus. The Garden was just a glimpse to the finality of the cross. Satan's perceived plan of defeat through death would allow each reader the freedom to step into what ultimately fits. Him. Life Love.

Ever since the Garden of Eden we have been "broken." We were meant to live in the Garden with all the amenities it had. But curiosity killed the cat and behold Adam and Eve were kicked out of the Garden of Eden and thrown into the world of sin. But notice what God does. He supplied them with a sacrifice and God Himself clothed them. What a benevolent God to provide clothes for them. A sacrifice of an animal was necessary for clothes to cover them. Sounds like another person who became our lamb of God to cover our sins. The Lamb of God. Notice what Adam and Eve did during this event of God clothing them. Absolutely nothing. Just like Adam we do nothing but sin during the salvation experience.

If you have ever felt "broken" then this song is for you. I bet Adam and Eve were in need of this song. God took Adam and Eve's sins and turned it into a blessing. My favorite artist is Julie Miller. She has been through a lot.

We are all broken creatures. Everybody struggles. Beware of the believer who says Praise God, my child is staying out late and drinking and driving. Beware of these Christians who never have a bad day. They are what I call super fake believers. Maybe they have just gotten some bad doctrine. You know the kind I am thinking of. In goes a quarter and out comes their desired product. My God is into taking broken things in our lives and refining us through the difficult times. God isn't a sugar daddy. He is God Almighty and is interested in the here and now and future. It is called the sanctification process. It is in these dark times that He grows us. We may hate this process, but when it is stripped away He has done an incredible work in and through us.

What do you do during the difficult day? Sometimes I do nothing. At other times I spring into action and do superman moves. Oh, when it comes to our kids, we will stop at nothing to bypass the pain and suffering. It is in the fire that we grow.

Isaiah 48:10"Behold, I have refined you, but not as silver I tried you in the furnace of affliction." (ESV)1Thessalonians 5:23a " Now may the God of peace sanctify you completely…" (ESV)

Broken Things
Written and sung by
Julie Miller

You can have my heart
Tough it isn't new
It's been used and abused
And only comes in blue
It's been down a long road
And it got dirty along the way
If I give it to you will you make it clean
And wash the shame way

You can have my heat
If you don't mind broken things
You can have my life if you don't mind these tears

Well I heard that you make all things new

We need to be on watch to see we are not being led astray by Satan. He is a real viable deity that is like "a thief who only comes to steal, kill, and destroy." (John 10:10, ESV) If we think he runs around in a little red outfit with horns on both sides of his head, we are very wrong. He is much smarter than that. Scripture says

2Corinthians 11:14a "...for even Satan disguises himself as an angel of light" (ESV) Once again I am ministered by music. Read these words. They are gut level honest.

The Devil Is An Angel
Lyrics and sung by Julie Miller

Well, you look just like an angel, you sound so bright and true,
You seem so sweet coming down my street,
but the devil is an angel too.
Somehow you seem familiar-haven't I seen you before?
Got a different name, but is it the same old
heartache coming 'round my door, my door?
Got one hand on my shoulder' you keep one behind your back,
I'm going to need some identification,
baby, before I let you unpack

Psalm 104:b
*"You are clothed with splendor and majesty, covering
yourself with light as with a garment." (ESV)*

We have an adversary. His name is Satan, the evil one or devil. He was a rejected angel, cast from heaven. Could you imagine what heaven was/is like? Talk about the all-you-can-eat buffet. The closest I can get to heaven's food is On The Border 's sizzling fahitas with extra sour cream, onions, and shredded cheddar cheese. And several diet cokes to wash it all down with.

What part do we play in the salvation experience? We sin. Plain and simple. We sin. When we do accept Christ and His spotless sacrifice, it is God who saves us, not us.

How benevolent is God. After Adam and Eve sinned and were hiding from God, He was so good to them. He Himself made something for each of them to wear. Was He mad? I doubt it. Disappointed. Maybe. God turned this setback into a comeback. Satan would not and never will win against God. He could have abandoned them for their sin. But He loves us too much to let us wander around in our muck and mire.

Isaiah 61:10 b "...for He has clothed me with garments of salvation." (ESV) This is big, who clothes us with garments of salvation? God does. We don't do it ourselves. God does it. Who saves us? We may spend years and years looking for God. We were lost, not Him. He alone is our salvation. We cannot in all actuality save ourselves. It is interesting that the word, garment, is used here. Remember the garments used by Adam and Eve were simply fig leaves. Then after the sacrifice used was a lamb and a lamb's wool clothing is lot more comfortable that a fig leaf. Is that a caring God or what?

God could have left them in the Garden in shame but He didn't. No He took the time to sacrifice a lamb; doesn't this sound familiar? An unblemished lamb was sacrificed and was used to "cover" or used to atone for their sin. All of heaven anticipated in looking to the cross for its redemption. It started in the Garden and finished at the cross.

What is our place in the salvation process? We do nothing but sin. Salvation is of God, not us. Redemption is about Christ. No us. But here's the kicker. God leaves it all to us. He is not a pushy God. He doesn't railroad us into something we don't want.

No, He is a gentleman. Only go into a relationship when we are ready He also is a patient God. He will wait for us until the day we die. That is faithful and loving Savior.

Job was an incredible man of God. God let Satan sift him in every area of his life. Let's take that in for a moment. His family, job, cattle, his health and yet God said to him in Job 13:15a "though he slay me, I will hope in him..."(ESV)

If I had lost everything as Job had, I would not be so faithful and upbeat. Think about losing everything. Your family, livelihood, and health. I don't know about you but I would want answers. I don't think I could have responded the way Job did. I. love how Job responded. Check it out. "Job 19:25a "For I know that my Redeemer lives..." (ESV)

Redeemer
Lyrics and sung by
Nicole C. Mullen

Who taught the sun
Where to stand in the morning
And who taught the ocean
You can only come this far
And who showed to moon
Where to hide till evening
Whose words alone can
Catch a falling star

Well I know my Redeemer lives
I know my Redeemer lives
All of creation testifies
This life within me cries

Job 13:15a
Though he slay me, I will hope in him..."(ESV)

The Lord only disciplines those who are His children. He cannot let them live lives unto themselves. If he did not love us and want to grow us, He would let us go to Satan's playground. As the verse above says, though He may slay us, our hope is in Him. Sometimes some people think God is vending machine. In goes the money or request and out comes our desired outcome. After all, we put the money in. But God is so much more powerful than this coke machine mentality. Sometimes abuses happen. Accidents occur. Diseases are terminal. I know a gal who has never had a life alternating event. She brags that the key to her good fortune is loving the Lord and living right. Heaven help her faith when, not if, but when a tragedy occurs. She is robbing God of His omnificence. It has become on what she does instead of letting God do His thing. How will her faith survive a close relative's death?

Psalm 20:4 "May he grant you your heart's desire and fulfill all your plans." (ESV)

Jeremiah 29: 11 "For I know the plans I have for you, declares the Lord, plans for welfare and not for evil, to give you a future, to give you a future a hope." (ESV)

Think about your favorite verse. Think why you like/love that verse. Nine times out of ten, it is an encouraging word. One way to overcome obstacles in our lives is to memorize scripture. When I ran the marathon I said Philippians 4:13 over and over during the race. It became my mantra. I ran the entire race. No walking at all. The most I had run before the marathon was 6 miles. What got me through? Love. I was running for my dearly departed prayer partner and best friend who died a year earlier. When training fails, love will get you through.

I would like to close with probably one of my favorite artists. I've used her throughout this book. If you wonder how God feels about us going outside the parameters of His will, just listen to Twila's words. He sees us as beautiful and can and will work through us as we grow in Him. I heard a preacher say one time that he did not want to be put up on a shelf because of an indiscretion during his ministry. I could not disagree more. What about David and Bathsheba or Saul/Paul? What about Rahab, Moses, etc. To say we are above all that because we are super duper believers is a lie. God doesn't use the I-have-it-all-together believers. No, He uses the sinful individuals, Is that a fact?

Yes, that is a fact. Can He use me and you? Twila thinks so .Let's end with her song. Be encouraged

How Beautiful
Written and sung by Twila Paris

How beautiful the hands that served
The wine and the bread and the sons of the earth
How beautiful the feet that walked
The long dusty roads and the hill to the cross.

How beautiful, how beautiful
How beautiful is the body of Christ

How beautiful, the heart that bled
That took all my sin and bore it instead

When we "wear" Christ we are doing God's work. God is interested in every detail of our lives. Why is that? Because God will use every inch of our lives. That gives me hope. Hope as mourning for our loved ones who have passed on. I use to buy suckers, tootsie pops. They were Martha's favorite. I took her some every time I saw her. It is funny but I still eat "our" favorite candy. It makes me feel closer or that I haven't forgotten her. I will never forget her. God knows our heart. Why not celebrate our loved one's life? Grieve on your own time table. There are no set rules in mourning. God grades on the curve. He has been through everything we are going through. He can turn anything and anyone into His servants. God sees us as beautiful. And heaven forbid without makeup. In sweats. No socks. He can use us wherever we are. And whenever He wants to isn't it time we stop dressing up death. Let's let God clothe us in Him. Life. Love.

Printed in the United States
by Baker & Taylor Publisher Services